Original title:
The Scarf's Embrace

Copyright © 2025 Creative Arts Management OÜ
All rights reserved.

Author: Thomas Sinclair
ISBN HARDBACK: 978-1-80586-049-5
ISBN PAPERBACK: 978-1-80586-521-6

Softened Silhouette

In winter's chill, I wrapped it tight,
A tangled mess, oh what a sight!
With every twist, I lost my way,
A cotton snake, come out to play.

Around my neck, it took a trip,
Choking out a hopeful quip.
A fashionista, I am not,
More like a clown in a tight spot.

It slipped and slid, a dance of grace,
Became a silly, warm embrace.
With every turn, it felt alive,
A playful knot, did I survive?

Oh, how it flops with every breeze,
A trusty friend that aims to please.
In every hug, it wobbles free,
A cozy joke, a sight to see.

Cloistered from the Cold

A twist of fabric, snug and tight,
It wraps around with all its might.
The winter wind can howl and scream,
But I'm cocooned, living the dream!

My buddies laugh, they think I'm mad,
Wearing this layer, oh so glad.
They joke I'm lost in fashion's stew,
Yet I'm just warm, unlike you too!

Emblems of Shelter

When snowflakes fall and chill the air,
I wear my shield with flair and care.
It flaps and dances, oh what a show,
   Like a peacock in winter's glow!

Friends tease me, saying I'm a clown,
In bright colors, I won't back down.
But cozy vibes are hard to beat,
   Who needs a coat? I'll just be sleek!

The Wrap of Remembrance

Once a drape of grandma's past,
It holds her hugs, so warm and vast.
With every loop, I laugh and spin,
A tapestry of giggles within!

Mismatched patterns, a glorious sight,
Each squishy fold brightens the night.
With every wear, her spirit winks,
And in my heart, her memory blinks!

Forgotten Stories in Cotton

In a drawer, it lay so meek,
A dust bunny of fashion's peak!
I claim it back, a newfound friend,
It whispers tales that never end!

Each twist confesses snippets bold,
Adventures waiting to be told.
Wrapped up, I strut with style and flair,
A cotton saga in frosty air!

Breath of the Weave

In a closet, it sneezes, so bold,
A swirl of threads, tales untold.
Hitchhiking on necks, what a sight,
Tickling noses, oh what a fright!

Colors collide, a dance so bright,
Tangled and twisted, a comical plight.
Worn by the dog, now that's a show,
What is fashion? Who even knows?

Emblem of Togetherness

Wrapped up snug like a burrito,
Huddling together, 'fore we go.
A mishap on dates, oh what a flair,
Forgotten warmth covering despair.

Pals in patterns, silly delight,
Fuzzy companions in morning light.
They giggle and wiggle, on they prance,
With every twist, they make you dance!

Embracement of Colors

A riot of hues, bright and bold,
They argue on who's the best to hold.
With polka dots and stripes galore,
Chasing the sunlight, always wanting more.

Wrapped around shoulders, a jolly sight,
Playing peek-a-boo from left to right.
Fashion faux pas, but who gives a hoot?
Life's too short, let colors root!

Layers of Laughter

Worn in layers, piled up high,
A mountain of fabric, oh me, oh my!
Trying to ride a bike, what a scene,
Who knew a wrap could be so mean?

Every twist brings giggles galore,
A jester's hat? I'll wear it for sure!
In windswept chaos, we frolic and spin,
Laughter wraps round, timeless grin!

Serenity in Stitches

In tangled yarn, I see my fate,
A cozy mess, oh what a state!
A loop here, a twist over there,
My knitting skills? Well, they're quite rare.

The cat thinks it's a game to play,
Pouncing on yarn, then running away.
I laugh and cry in equal measure,
My hobby's both a pain and treasure.

Unraveled Connections

I knitted a gift for my dear mate,
But the pattern might just tempt a fate.
It turned into a hat, or so I claimed,
When really, it was just quite maimed.

Threads loop and twist in wild delight,
Each stitch I make is a comic sight.
Friends gather round with curious stares,
At my creations, all awkward flares.

Softness Surrounds

In a basket of fluff and colors bright,
I create shapes, a whimsical sight.
But my project's a blob, just for fun,
Is it a monster or a soft bun?

With every purl and with every knit,
I chuckle at what I've made of it.
A cozy companion, for laughter's sake,
Turns me into a stitchy flake.

Cascade of Comfort

On my needles, a rainbow flows,
But what it becomes, nobody knows.
It starts as a scarf, turns into a shawl,
   Or is it a blanket? I can't recall.

Laughter echoes as loops interlace,
With each tangled thread, I misplace.
Comfort wrapped in a crazy embrace,
Who knew crafts could be such a race?

Warmth in Every Fold

A twist of fabric, snug and neat,
Bright colors dance, oh what a treat!
Wrapped around like a cozy hug,
Laughing at winter's frosty tug.

In every layer, joy's concealed,
Fashioned snug, it's quite the shield.
Flapping like a flag, proud and bold,
In winds that shout, it still won't fold.

Cloth and Care

A gentle swirl around my neck,
Makes me giggle, oh what the heck!
It teases me, this fabric friend,
Pretending it knows how to bend.

Stitches humming, laughter sings,
Cozy vibes and silly things.
As I trip, it seems to cheer,
This playful wrap, I hold so dear.

Weaving Whimsy

Laughter caught in threads of dye,
Tickles me as I wander by.
A loop, a knot, a twist, a turn,
It plays with style, oh how to learn!

With every sway, a chuckle comes,
A fabric tale that giggles, hums.
Dancing in the chilly breeze,
This happy wrap is sure to please.

Quilt of the Heart

A patchwork blend of love and cheer,
Stitched together, everyone near.
With every fold, a story spun,
In playful threads, we laugh and run.

Woven snug, no cold can bite,
Embracing warmth, all feels just right.
It's more than cloth, a bond that grows,
In every tuck, the laughter flows.

Whispers of Fabric

A fabric flutters, oh so sly,
It tickles my neck, no need to tie.
In windy gusts, it starts to play,
I chase it down, oh what a fray!

It wraps around like a playful cat,
Tug at one end, it's a soft spat.
Each twist and turn, a dance to see,
Leaving me laughing, oh the glee!

Threads of Warmth

A tangle of threads, a bundle of cheer,
It hugs me close, my warm souvenir.
Knitted with love, a colorful spree,
I wear it boldly, it fits like a bee.

In coffee shops, I sip with flair,
My neck adorned, I'm a stylish affair.
It spills its yarn, a friendly tease,
I laugh and boast, it's sure to please!

Embraced by Wool

The woolly delight, a cozy embrace,
It wobbles about, in this silly race.
With every twist, I crack a smile,
It keeps me warm, in fanciful style.

At dinner parties, it steals the show,
My lively wrap, with its funny glow.
It makes me trip, in the wittiest way,
Yet I wear it proudly, come what may!

A Tapestry of Comfort

A patchwork wonder, each stitch a giggle,
My treasure's alive, as it starts to wiggle.
Every hue tells a story of fun,
I drape it around, like a playful pun.

In quirky cafés, I dance with flair,
My silly wrap, a comedic affair.
It spins and sways, a partner in crime,
Together we laugh, in rhythm and rhyme!

Textured Tranquility

In a twist of fabric, muffs the breeze,
I trip on my own style, oh what a tease!
Wrapped up like a burrito, snug and tight,
Laughing at the mirror, what a sight!

My edges are frayed, a devil-may-care,
Like spaghetti tangled in an old chair.
Each thread a giggle, colors collide,
Fashion's a circus, I take it in stride!

Layers of Life

Put on my layers, a tower of pride,
Like a sandwich stacked high, I can't fit inside!
Quirky and cozy, with patterns that clash,
Dancing like a fool, making quite the splash!

A squeeze and a shuffle, I'm lost in my gear,
Look like a marshmallow, but full of good cheer.
With each zany wrap, I feel like a queen,
This wardrobe's a party, if you know what I mean!

Enfolded Stories

My layers narrate tales of mishaps and fun,
Each stitch is a memory, second to none.
I wear my own history, both bright and absurd,
Like a fashion show mishap, all funny and blurred!

The tales I carry in each cozy fold,
From spills on the carpet, to secrets retold.
Draped in my fabric, I wink at the past,
A treasure of laughter, I'm stitched up to last!

The Embrace in Every Stitch

A cozy embrace, a hug from my coat,
Looks like a quilt that someone forgot to note!
Each fiber holds secrets, both silly and wise,
I'm dressed like a puzzle with mismatched ties!

With every loop, a chuckle I find,
A couture catastrophe, but I don't mind.
Swaddled in laughter, I'm ready for fun,
Fashion so funky, I'm second to none!

Tapestry of Touch

In a tangled heap, it fell from the chair,
Like a jigsaw puzzle, it's everywhere!
Around my neck, it takes a spin,
I wear it proudly like a squirrel with a grin.

It tickles my nose, a feathery tease,
Wrapped up in colors, I feel the breeze.
My cat makes a throne of that fabric wide,
Claiming the warmth, like it's a joyride.

A dance with the fabric, I trip and I sway,
It's not just a scarf, it's a playful fray.
Knots and curls, a sight to behold,
Each twist tells a story, both silly and bold.

Layers of Love

In layers like cake, it wraps me with glee,
I'm a walking dessert, sweet as can be!
My friends take a photo, they can't get enough,
'Is that frosting?' they ask, 'or just too much fluff?'

The chaos of colors, a whimsical sight,
Matching my socks, it's a wild delight!
In winter's embrace, I'm a marshmallow bright,
Waddling around, oh, what a funny sight!

When it slips and it slides, it brings on some cheer,
Like a runaway puppy, in frigid frontier.
Yet in the frosty air, I stand tall and proud,
An artist's mishap, wrapped under a cloud.

Gentle Ties

A gentle connection, it makes me feel good,
Knotting together, like starlings in hood.
It wraps 'round my head like a goofy old hat,
While I chase my own shadow, it's always a spat!

Adventures do bloom, when the wind takes a turn,
Each swirl and each gust, teaches me to learn.
At times it's a fling, a sweet game of tag,
How it dances away, oh, let's not wag!

With a wink and a curl, it hugs me just right,
A chuckle escapes, what a comical sight!
Each journey we take, is a laugh and a tease,
Forever entwined, in a twist of the breeze.

The Warm Weave

A tapestry warms, but also can play,
In a jumbled heap on a grand ballet.
It swirls like a dancer, oh what a spree,
Though I trip on the end, it laughs back at me!

When it wraps 'round my head, I'm a fashion faux pas,
Like a cozy burrito, with all the strange flaws.
I boast of my style with a wink and a grin,
In the zoo of my closet, I feel like a king!

As I strut down the street, it flutters with pride,
Each fluttering flap is a whimsical ride.
With a heart full of chuckles and warmth in my chest,
I embrace this weirdness, it's my very best jest!

Emotions in Elegance

A twist here, a flip there, so chic,
This fabric spins tales, oh what a sneak!
It cuddles your neck, whispers delight,
Keeping you warm and soaring in flight.

With patterns so bold, who needs a crown?
We strut like royalty, never a frown.
In colors that clash, we find our fun,
This playful attire, our victory won.

Draped around shoulders, it teems with flair,
It's not just a cloth, it's pure debonair!
Watch the kiddos giggle, they wrap it right tight,
It's a superhero cape, what a sight!

Even the dog gets tangled in grace,
Dressed up in knots, he's part of the race.
With a wag and a jump, he joins in the game,
Oh, the giggles we share, never the same!

Draped in Memories

In the corner, it hangs, a relic of cheer,
Whispers of laughter, friends gathered near.
A splash of old style, it sways with pride,
Every fold recalls a joyride!

When the pie falls flat, and the wine spills too,
This trusty companion will know what to do.
It's a napkin, a flag, and sometimes a scarf,
It catches our quirks, it's the one we laugh!

Each wrinkle a greeting, each spot a tale,
From picnics to parties, on every scale.
With secrets concealed in its colorful seams,
This cloth is adventure, birthed from dreams!

Hues of Hope

A splash of brilliant red, like ketchup on fries,
Yellow as sunshine, sparking up smiles!
Green for the envy that follows our flair,
These shades come alive, they dance in the air.

The playful stripes sport a game of their own,
A match for the socks that desperately moan.
Patterns collide, a raucous delight,
Chaos in fabric can't be kept right!

Our pockets are stuffed with snacks for the ride,
Popcorn and giggles, nothing to hide.
Watch as we strut through the streets with a grin,
In hues of pure hope, let the fun begin!

Fabric of Friends

A patchwork of laughter stitched tight with glue,
Through stitches and seams, our bond's ever true.
With buttons of joy and zippers of glee,
We wrap up our stories, just you and me.

From sleepovers wild to the coffee shop haze,
This fabric binds us in unforgettable ways.
We drape our wishes, and dreams on the line,
This textile of friendship, aged like good wine.

As we spill our secrets, each tear is a patch,
Matching socks in mischief, oh what a catch!
Every tear and mend tells a quirky tale,
In the fabric of friendship, we always prevail.

Cozy Elegance

In winter's bite, we wrap our neck,
With colors bright, a lovely deck.
Knitted tight, not a loose thread,
A cozy hug that's far from dread.

A fashion choice, not just for warmth,
Twisting tails, a joyful swarth.
In café light, we sip and grin,
Wrapped in style, let the fun begin!

Laughter flows like tea from pots,
While tangled knots bring cheery thoughts.
A swirling dance of fabric grace,
As friends unite in scarf embrace!

So many ways to tie the ends,
In stripes and polka dots, we blend.
A playful twist, a cheeky flair,
Life's too short for dull affair.

Enveloped by Time

Threads of laughter from days gone by,
Weaving tales that make us cry.
A tangled twist of memories shared,
Wrap us softly, showing we cared.

Upon the neck, stories unfold,
Each loop a treasure, each fold pure gold.
In chilly air, our warmth is found,
With every knot, a smile unbound!

Time's embrace, a cheeky wink,
In bright hues, we pause to think.
Life's a laugh, with style and flare,
Embrace the quirks, toss worry in air!

Fables spun from fibers bright,
Celebrating joy in fabric's flight.
In every swipe, a giggle glows,
As our charming weariness shows!

Fabrics of Solitude

Alone at home, tucked in a throw,
My scarf and me—quite the show!
We've shared secrets and cozy nights,
Watching clouds and city lights.

In quiet moments, it's quite the thrill,
A fortress snug, with a playful spill.
Stitches whisper, stories foiled,
In solitude, our friendship coiled.

A cat might purr, a mug might clink,
Yet nothing beats this linen link.
We laugh at trends, old styles cobbled,
Who needs a crowd? We'll be bobbled!

So here we lie, without a care,
Wrapped in warmth, beyond compare.
In comfort found, we slyly plot,
The quirkiest adventures on the spot!

Ribbons of Reflection

Twirling ribbons dance on air,
Each one a tale of smart repair.
Reflecting laughs from days gone past,
In colors bright, forever cast.

With a flourish here and a knot so tight,
We twine our stories, silly and bright.
From silly gags to heartfelt chats,
This woven world's where laughter spats.

Rain or shine, our moods untangle,
In every twist, new smiles dangle.
With layers deep of humor's zest,
In threads of joy, we find our nest!

So grab your lengths, let giggles soar,
In every wrap, we'll laugh some more.
In life's mad dance, we find a way,
With ribbons bright, we brave each day!

Love's Touch in Twill

Beneath the twill, a sneaky twist,
A tug of yarn, my neck's insist.
It flutters here and wriggles there,
Like a tiny pet, it shows its flair.

A dance of colors, wild and bright,
It mocks my efforts, gives me fright.
With every knot, it tends to tease,
A fashion foe, it does as it please.

It wraps me snug, then sneaks away,
In public, I look slightly cray.
But oh, what joy it brings at night,
This cheeky wrap, my heart's delight.

So here's to twill and warmth combined,
In every fold, hilarity twined.
My love for it, quite hard to shake,
In its embrace, oh what a break!

Comfort in the Knots

A knot so tight, it's quite the feat,
It hugs my neck like a warm treat.
But sometimes it's a tangled mess,
I look a fright, but I must confess.

In chilly air, it stands its ground,
When I trip, it makes a sound.
"Watch your step!" it seems to shout,
This silly wrap, oh what a clout.

With every twist, it brings a smile,
A cozy hug, it's worth the while.
Though friends may laugh in sheer delight,
I'm snug and warm, so it's all right.

So here's to knots that make us grin,
Together we'll laugh, we just can't win.
Comfort found in every fold,
A bond that's worth its weight in gold.

Warmth Woven Deep

In chilly dawn, it claims its space,
A snuggly shield, my cozy grace.
But on the train, it starts to roam,
My neighbor's snack, it calls it home.

With every slip, it flits away,
A playful dance, a yarn ballet.
"Hey, that's mine!" I huff and pout,
But deep inside, it makes me shout.

Its hues of joy, they shout "Be bold!"
In every stitch, I find the gold.
Though sometimes it gets stuck in ties,
I wear it proud, to everyone's surprise.

So here's to warmth that likes to play,
In quirky fashions, come what may.
A woven warmth, so full of cheer,
This wrap of fun, forever near.

The Cloak of Connection

A cloak of laughter, twirls around,
In everyday mischief, it's quite profound.
It flares out wide at the silliest times,
Becoming a circus, with over-the-top rhymes.

It whispers secrets in a playful tone,
This fabric friend, I've never outgrown.
With every swing, a story's spun,
I trip and tumble, but laugh, oh what fun!

At parties, it captures every glance,
With all its patterns, it leads the dance.
The louder I laugh, the more it shows,
This quirky cloak, it surely knows.

So here's to the joys of fabric friends,
In twists and turns, the fun never ends.
With every hug, it wraps me tight,
In a playful bond, my heart takes flight.

Stitches of Affection

In a pile of wool I found,
A rebel knot, quite round.
It twisted with a cheeky glee,
Dancing yarn, come play with me.

I wrapped it tight around my neck,
It grinned like a merry wreck.
Onlookers laughed, what a sight!
Warmed my heart, brought sheer delight.

No fashion sense, I cast away,
It's cozy, fun, and here to stay.
A warm embrace from stitch to stitch,
Oh, how I love this silly glitch!

In vibrant hues, it taunts the cold,
A silly tale it has retold.
With knots and loops, I set the pace,
In every bobble, joy we chase.

Snuggled in Threads

A tangled bundle on my lap,
Looks just like a furry trap.
Last week's fashion, quite a fail,
Yet cozy wins in giddy tale.

It tickles me, the yarn so fine,
Laughter bubbles like sweet wine.
Who knew warmth could be so bold?
A wiggly faux, a sight to behold!

I sport it like a badge of fun,
Inspired by a cartoon run.
Each twist and turn a playful jest,
In this fabric, I feel blessed.

With every loop, a giggly sigh,
This silly scarf, I'm not shy.
It wraps around, a hug, a tease,
In threads of joy, I find my ease.

Cascade of Textures

A fiber festival, oh what cheer,
With colors that bring joy so near.
I twirl and swish, a fabric dance,
Who knew yarn could lead a romance?

Each scrunch and squish, a melody,
My quirky cloak sings happily.
A texture splash, what a sight,
My wardrobe's joy in merry light!

It jingles with each little hitch,
A playful swing, not a stitch to itch.
Not your ordinary winter gear,
This joyous thread brings a big cheer!

A cascade of laughs, watch it flow,
In this whirlwind, laughter grows.
With every layer, a bit more fun,
Draped in threads, adventures spun!

Breezy Comforts

A chill in the air, I proudly strut,
In a misfit wrap, unintentionally cut.
Flapping like flags in a playful breeze,
This quirky layer aims to please.

It dances wildly, chuckles high,
Who knew comfort could reach the sky?
With silly bows and mismatched patterns,
It surely wins, while laughter scatters.

My friends all mock, but I don't care,
For in this wrap, I'm floating air.
Every gust a giggle, I embrace,
Soft and silly, the perfect space.

So here I twirl, a cape of glee,
In breezy comfort, wild and free.
With every turn, I spin my tale,
In chuckles spun, I happily sail.

Threads that Bind

In a twist and a turn, it's caught my chair,
A trap for my feet, a hug of despair.
It jumps, it dances, it twirls with glee,
A rebel of fabric, oh set it free!

It snags in the door, oh what a delight,
It tickles my ankles, a humorous sight.
Laughter erupts at my fashion faux pas,
As I trip and I stumble, oh look at that scar!

Unruly and wild, it's a silky affair,
Popcorn at the movies? No, it's stuck in my hair!
Yet somehow it clings, my flamboyant friend,
Together we'll laugh, 'til the very end.

With patterns so bright, it's a riot of style,
Bringing joy and giggles, all the while.
A friend on my journey, it can't be denied,
In the chaos of life, we're happily tied.

Embrace of the Elements

Whirling through breezes, it flutters with flair,
A dance with the sun, in the wild open air.
Chased by the raindrops, it dodges and weaves,
Each twist and each turn, a playful reprieve.

Worn by the clumsies, it's tangled for sure,
A stylish tornado, oh what a allure!
As puddles it splashes, I giggle and squeal,
A whirlwind of laughter, my fashion ideal.

Caught on the branches, it grips like a friend,
A game of peekaboo, where will it end?
It launches with leaves on a mischievous spree,
Every snag tells a tale, oh bring joy to me!

In seasons of change, it shines bright and bold,
A story of laughter, forever retold.
So here's to the skies, the storms, and the sun,
In this silly embrace, we melt into fun.

Wrap of Warmth

Oh, this wrap of laughter, so soft and so wide,
It laps at my sides like a merry-go-ride.
Snatching up cookies, it's learned how to bake,
This delicious companion, oh make no mistake!

At dinner it joins in, a wild buffet pass,
It swallows my dinner, I blush and I laugh.
It seems to conspire to grow wider and round,
A merry balloon that can't settle down!

With spaghetti entwined, it's a sight to behold,
I wear it with pride, though it's saucy and bold.
A bib and a cloak, it's a duel I can't face,
In this funny wrap, life's a chaotic race.

Be it summer or winter, it's always a hit,
With patterns so quirky, and colors that fit.
It hugs me with joy, as I dance and I twirl,
In this warm, silly hug, let's give life a whirl!

Threads of Affection

With threads interwoven, hilarity does bloom,
Each twist and each turn creates laughter and room.
A hug that's contagious, it spreads with a grin,
Silly little stitches, oh let the fun begin!

Wrap it around you, a dance in the night,
It flops and it flutters, what a goofy sight!
As I trip on my heels, it's enough to make cheer,
For whom do I blame? Oh, the wrap's not very clear!

In moments we fumble, it trips me yet more,
Like a playful pet, it rolls on the floor.
Each tug and each pull, leads to giggles galore,
These threads of affection mean we're never a bore.

So here's to our antics, once tangled, once neat,
Each laugh a reminder, life's silly and sweet.
With threads that unite us, let's frolic and play,
In laughter we thrive, come what may!

Cloaked in Warmth

A bundle of fabric wrapped around tight,
A fashion statement, oh what a sight!
Keeps me warm when the cold winds bite,
Like a big hug, furry and bright.

Twists and twirls around my neck,
I feel like a cozy shipwreck.
Worn too long? A bit of a speck,
Yet, it's still my favorite check!

Threads of Togetherness

In a million colors, oh how they dance,
Weaving stories, giving warmth a chance.
When I trip and fall, it's part of the romance,
With fabric flying, it's all part of the prance.

A tangled mess on laundry day,
I tug and pull, here goes my sway.
With every knot, a price to pay,
But I wear it proud, come what may!

Entwined in Care

Laughter echoes, as the fabric plays,
It twirls and spins in winding ways.
A blanket on my lap, where silliness stays,
Or a makeshift cape on a dreary day.

Pulling it tighter, I pretend to fly,
In my cozy fortress, I reach for the sky.
Though my cat thinks it's a comfy pie,
I'm just a superhero, oh me, oh my!

Shields of Softness

Caught in the fluff of a cozy affair,
A fabric fortress, without a care.
Hiding snacks from the glaring stare,
What a delight, this soft layer's flair!

With patterns that clash and colors that sing,
It's battle-ready for whatever life brings.
Dodge a sneeze or a sudden fling,
In this warm cocoon, I'm ruling like a king!

Swaying in the Breeze

When I put you on, I feel quite grand,
With tassels swaying, a dance at hand.
Neighbors chuckle, then start to stare,
   As I twirl like I just don't care.

Colors clash, a riot of hues,
Feeling chic in my whimsy shoes.
But caught in wind, oh what a sight,
   I'm a fabric kite, ready for flight!

With each gust, I flap and flail,
   Is this fashion or a comedy tale?
Strangers laugh, they can't help but tease,
   As I struggle to stay upright with ease!

In my cozy wrap that's two sizes too wide,
I'm feeling fine, looking in my stride.
Each step is merry, each swing is a whirl,
   My woven adventure, a fabric swirl!

Woven Memories

Tangled threads, oh what a scene,
Each stitch a story, some quite obscene.
A mix of patterns, a riot of flair,
I'm the life of the party, I swear!

Vintage vibes in a neon glow,
At brunch, I'm the star of the show.
Pancakes are served, syrup will miss,
When I lean in for that buttery kiss!

Through laughs and spills, I've seen it all,
From wedding dances to a field trip ball.
I'm a quirky reminder of joys we claim,
Wrapping laughter in timeless fame.

With my fabric tales that twist and fold,
I'm the memory keeper, bold and old.
In every crease, a cheerful cheer,
Woven in warmth, my love is near!

The Velvet Wrap

With velvet softness, I glide and sway,
Prancing about in a clumsy ballet.
Friends are giggling, it's hard to contain,
As I strut like a peacock, losing my brain!

A fashionable cloak, but where's my grace?
My elegance feels like a low-speed chase.
Caught on a doorknob, I pull and I twist,
A fabric fumble that can't be missed!

In the café, I'm the quirky delight,
My bouncy demeanor gives quite a fright.
Spilling my coffee, oh what a show,
The velvet saga, it steals the glow!

So here I am, in a puddle of cream,
The life of the party, or so it would seem.
Wrapped in joy, though frazzled and fried,
Each velvet embrace is my hilarious ride!

Caress of the Chill

With winter's breath, I zip and pull,
The chill is sharp, my style is full.
But—oops! I slipped on a patch of ice,
My fashion statement, not quite so nice!

I shiver and giggle, oh what a blunder,
A flurry of laughs and a little thunder.
Bouncing back up, I wrap up tight,
Like a bundle of joy, ready for flight!

Each frostbitten breeze, a playful tease,
And when I'm bundled, I'm sure to freeze.
Yet in this fray, I manage a grin,
With layers of warmth, let the fun begin!

So here's to the cold and the laughter it brings,
Like a snowman's dance and all silly things.
Wrapped up snug, till the sun comes back,
I'll wear my chilly joy without any lack!

Fabrication of Feelings

A twist and a tug, oh what joy,
This fabric won't let me go, my boy!
Around my neck, it starts to twist,
I swear it's got a mind, it must resist!

It tickles my chin, gives my hair a fright,
Who knew this cloth could spark a fight?
Always falling off when I run,
Maybe it just wants to have some fun!

Feather-light whispers, a gentle tease,
Half a hug, or was that a squeeze?
Wrapping me up, it plays the game,
Yet when it slips, who's to blame?

I laughed so hard, I nearly fell,
Caught in the fabric's jolly spell.
In each fray, a hint of glee,
This playful cloth just loves to be free!

Cozy Binds

Oh cozy wraps that twirl and twine,
Turn work to jokes, every single time.
A pliable friend, it rides the breeze,
Chasing happiness with greatest ease.

Around my shoulders, it holds me tight,
Yet lets me out just when I might.
A mischief-maker? Perhaps it's true,
But even in chaos, I still love you!

When I'm lazy, it knows the score,
To be my blanket or just explore.
Rolling me up like a burrito bless,
We giggle and squirm in a cozy mess.

It may be a wrap, but it's more than that,
A playful prank, a loyal spat.
Always ups for a silly tease—
My fabric buddy puts me at ease!

Entangled Souls

In a jumbled knot, what a sight to see,
My fabric friend is clingy as can be.
A playful twist and a swirl about,
Together we dance, let's give a shout!

Tugging here, tugging there, what a mess,
This cloth has skills, I must confess!
Like a hug that won't let go—
When I try to leave, it says, 'Oh no!'

With colors bright, and patterns wild,
This wrap's the jester, a playful child.
Bouncing off walls, swinging 'round chairs,
A camaraderie that simply declares!

In every fold, and creased delight,
Lies a friendship bound, oh so tight.
Come rain or shine, we share a laugh,
Two tangled souls, on a merry path!

Cloaked in Affection

I walk in this whimsy, oh what a treat,
This cloak of mine nibbles at my feet.
With pockets full of secrets to share,
Together we giggle, not a single care.

It spills all over, in colors so bright,
As if happy hues had taken flight.
When I leap for joy, it flops behind,
Is it friendship or just being blind?

With a swirl and a bounce, we're quite the pair,
In this fabric adventure, we're without a care.
Each trip and shuffle, a playful dance,
Around and around in a whimsical trance!

Laughter erupts at every turn,
A fabric fiesta that makes me yearn.
For in this fluff, there's nothing but cheer,
Cloaked in delight, my friend is near!

Knotted Memories

In the drawer, tangled thread,
Worn and twisted, colors fled.
A fashion statement, what a sight,
Wrapped around my cat at night.

Chasing dust bunnies, what a thrill,
With every tug, a gleeful spill.
My grandma's gift, from yesteryear,
Now a comedy, oh dear, oh dear!

At picnics, it kept me warm,
But tangled past a love's true charm.
Each knot a tale, a laugh, a cheer,
Memories bound, forever near.

So here's a tip, rather sage,
Don't wrap your gifts, that's the rage!
Just toss it in, let chaos reign,
Laughing at life, we'll dance in rain.

Threads of Time

A yarn unwinds through dark and light,
Each loop a giggle, tight or slight.
In fashion's name, I try to weave,
But end up tangled, oh I believe!

An old sweater, such a delight,
With sleeves so long, it's quite a sight.
When I wear it, arms look like wings,
A hurried flight of fashion flings!

At every party, I'm a hit,
With threads that snag on every bit.
Friends just chuckle, "Oh look at her!"
Part walking joke, part fashion blur.

I promise one day to untie,
These crazy knots, oh me, oh my!
But till that time, I'll let it be,
A comic tale of yarn and me.

The Ties That Keep

An old necktie upon my shelf,
Could tell a tale of its great self.
It danced with joy, it tied a bow,
Its colors shout in vibrant glow.

At family dinners, once so neat,
It slipped and slid, a grand old feat.
Spaghetti sauce now holds a place,
On that dear tie, my fashion grace.

It flung around while I had fun,
Made me a target, oh what a run!
With every slip, I laughed aloud,
A tie's proud boast, a silly crowd.

Though frayed and worn, it holds my heart,
Its stories spun with every part.
So here's to ties, both near and far,
That keep us close, our goofy star!

Silken Guardian

A fabric swatch, soft as a sigh,
Wrapped around me, oh my, oh my!
It billows here and sways so free,
Like an untrained puppy, wait and see.

In wind it flies, a grand parade,
A silken cape that's brightly made.
Spinning 'round, I lose my way,
A hero lost in fabric play.

It guards my shins, it hugs my waist,
And always leaves a ribboned trace.
My quirky outfit, what a blend,
Fashion faux pas, my wooly friend!

Yet in the chaos, I find my glee,
That playful spirit still lives in me.
So here's to fabric, wild and bright,
A guardian's laugh in every flight.

Tender Threads

In a twist of purple yarn,
Lies a tale that's quite bizarre.
It tangled up my cat one night,
Now he's a fashion superstar!

Puppies chew, and kittens climb,
A scarf became our family mime.
We laugh and trip in garish threads,
Woven joy, no fear it spreads.

Friends arrive with patterns wild,
They claim they're trendy, yet so mild.
Knitting needles dance in glee,
As they fashion hats for me!

Laughter echoes, stitches break,
All caught up in our scarf's quake.
Who knew fabric brought such fun?
In this game, we've all just won!

Woven Dreams

In a basket, colors play,
Knotted dreams that laugh all day.
I wore one draped like a cape,
Now I'm the neighborhood grape!

Sibling's closet, oh what a mess,
Tangled threads, a knit excess.
"Borrowed" styles, did I imply?
Not sure who's the thief, oh my!

A woven tale spun with guile,
Fuzzy fashion makes us smile.
Caught in a loop, we can't escape,
Who knew knitting could reshape?

With needles clacking, tales unfold,
Our wrapping game is never old.
Each stitch a laugh, a woven scheme,
Life's a yarn; a wacky dream!

Embrace of the Fabric

In the corner of the room,
Lies fabric causing all this doom.
It hugs me tight, I can't get free,
Who knew cloth could be so cheeky?

Friends arrive with blank stares,
"Is that a blanket, or a pair of shares?"
We laugh so hard, we start to wheeze,
Fabric phantoms dance with ease!

A scarf that laughs, a shirt that jokes,
They tickle me, oh what strokes!
In this comedy of knit,
Every cuddle feels like wit.

Genres clash, styles collide,
Yet we wear them with such pride.
Life's too short for fashion fuss,
With threads like these, it's always a plus!

Couture of Connection

A mismatch here, a swirl of flair,
My wardrobe's like a circus fair!
Pants are too short, and shirts too wide,
Yet I strut with confident pride.

My buddy's sweater, oversized,
It's like a hug that's not disguised.
We giggle as we trip and twirl,
In this fabric, we unfurl!

Couture moments, crazily spun,
Who knew style could be so fun?
With every stitch a shared delight,
Our story's woven, snug and bright.

Connection laced in every seam,
Together, living out the dream.
In this tapestry, we relate,
Every loop, a tale we create!

Harmonious Wrap

Around my neck it twirls with glee,
A fashion statement, can't you see?
It tickles my chin, oh what a tease,
And flutters in the wind; such a breeze!

Sometimes it hides, slips down with flair,
A mischievous prank—does it care?
It dances when I'm out on the street,
Making heads turn; oh what a feat!

It's soft, it's bright, a riot of hues,
When I wear it wrong, it gives me a snooze.
With patterns so wild, it gets in my way,
But I love it still, come what may!

Through laughs and stumbles, it knows me well,
My cosiest friend, with stories to tell.
In the morning rush or the evening's glow,
A partner in crime; I'm never alone!

Enveloping Emotions

It wraps me up like a warm, big hug,
While sipping coffee, it gives a shrug.
In chilly weather, it struts with pride,
Turning my frosty frown to a joyous ride!

At parties, it quips with a cheeky grin,
Just when I thought I might wear my sin.
Worn sideways or tangled, who even cares?
It's all in good fun, sharing laughs and stares.

A patchwork of joy, with stories so bright,
It gets in my soup at the silliest sight.
"Oh dear!" I proclaim with a giggle-filled sigh,
My snuggly companion, oh my, oh my!

Through all of life's mess, it's there by my side,
A quirky ensemble, my trusty pride.
It captures my laughter, my tears, and my cheer,
A woven adventure that's perfectly clear!

Breathable Bonds

Tossed in the air, it has a soft giggle,
Twisting and turning, oh what a wiggle!
It flops in the breeze like it's catching a ride,
With flair and with joy, it's my silly guide!

On breezy days, it knows how to play,
Hiding behind shades like a whimsical ray.
It wraps round my head, an impromptu crown,
And all of my worries just tumble down!

In sunshine and laughter, it dances along,
It's never quite serious; it sings me a song.
With every twist, a surprise it unveils,
My laughter cascades, and the happiness sails!

Through every mishap or quirky delight,
It keeps me from frump; oh what a sight!
A bundle of fun, a splendid embrace,
In all of my antics, it finds its own place!

Hands of Warmth

It grips my neck—not a chokehold, I swear!
More a gentle nudge, like love in the air.
With pockets of warmth, my style it supports,
Transforming my looks into laugh-filled reports!

It slips and it slides, a playful delight,
Gives my everyday jacket a friendly invite.
When it trips me up, we both laugh so hard,
My trusty companion, one silly bard!

Fashion faux pas? Oh, it doesn't agree,
It swirls in defiance, laughing with me.
Training my fashion sense, quite a feat,
When I wear it wrong, it's still pretty sweet!

At times it gets tangled, an unholy mess,
But with its embrace, I feel nothing less.
It's hands in the warmth of the giggles we make,
Whether I'm dancing or shaking with cake!

Silken Shadows

In the closet, lurking tight,
A prankster scarf, oh what a sight!
It slinks around with such great flair,
Causing chaos everywhere.

It wraps my neck, it tickles my chin,
With every twist, it pulls me in.
A fabric tease, it sways and spins,
In its embrace, where laughter begins.

When I take a step, it jumps and flops,
Like a playful pet that never stops.
With silly antics, it winks and grins,
My lively foe, where humor wins.

As it billows in the breeze so bold,
It's more than cloth, it's laughter gold.
In the dance of fashion, I must confess,
The best of times, with mischief's dress.

Hearth of Textiles

By the fire, a blanket sprawls,
But look! A scarf clings to the walls.
It steals the spotlight, still and sly,
Waiting for a chance to fly!

With every cup of cocoa sipped,
It twirls around like it has flipped.
Draped over chairs, it's plotting schemes,
A fabric jester, bursting dreams.

Friends gather 'round for toasty cheer,
Before they know it, here comes the queer!
The scarf leaps forth, wraps 'round their heads,
A woven joke from padded beds.

Shouting, laughing, what a sight!
As it dances in the warm twilight.
A cozy jester, always in play,
Spreading joy in its own way!

Cloak of Serenity

A cloak that whispers soft and low,
Yet sometimes it just wants to show!
It wraps me snug, a fashion tease,
Yet springs to life with playful ease.

One moment calm, a gentle breeze,
Next it flaps and tries to please.
With every wear, it takes a chance,
To join in on the silly dance.

On lazy days, I lounge about,
The cloak? It giggles, jumps, and shouts.
Such a comfort, yet mischief brews,
In cozy mayhem, it loves to snooze.

At dinner time, it drags the chair,
With guests who wear and laughter to share.
A cloak of calm, yet wild and free,
The best of both, a funny spree!

Dance of Colors

In colors bright, a canvas swirls,
A scarf that giggles as it twirls.
It wraps around, it spins and gleams,
A riot of fun, fulfilling dreams.

Pinks and blues, a vibrant blast,
It trips and stumbles, what a contrast!
A tapestry wearing a smile so wide,
With every flop, there's fun inside.

"Look at me!" it shouts with glee,
As I search for warmth, it won't let me be.
A waltz of patterns, laughter flows,
In the rhythm of fabric, hilarity grows.

At every party, it takes the stage,
Bouncing round like a joyful sage.
Colorful chaos, a vivid spree,
This joyful dance, just let it be!

Enfolded in Love

Wrapped around my neck so tight,
A silly knot, what a fright!
It slips and slides, oh what a tease,
Chasing it down like a lost sneeze.

In colors bright, like a rainstorm's hue,
It tickles my chin, who knew?
Each twist and turn a dance of fate,
I swear it might just be my date!

Through windy days, it flutters with glee,
A fashionista's flair, it thinks it's free.
With every laugh, it wraps just right,
Silly companion in day and night!

So here's to the rag, my fluffy friend,
With antics and mischief, it won't end.
Though tangled we are, in this bizarre race,
Together we bound in a funny embrace!

Stitches of Solace

A patchwork of laughs, quirky and bold,
Each stitch a story waiting to unfold.
It drapes upon me, a woven delight,
Whispering secrets, making things right.

Once lost in laundry, it played hide and seek,
Emerging from chaos, all wrinkled and bleak.
With patterns so wild, it cracks me up,
An unexpected joy in a teacup!

In sunny parks or rainy cafes,
It brings out my giggles in the silliest ways.
With each gentle tug, it's a playful tease,
A warm quilt of chuckles, a cozy breeze.

Oh stitches of solace, you truly amaze,
In laughter and warmth, we dance through the haze.
As the world spins by with a curious glance,
Together we twirl, in an unruly dance!

Woven Memories

Threads of laughter entwined so tight,
Riding the waves of a whimsical flight.
In every loop, a giggle tucked in,
Creating a tapestry where fun must begin.

Frolicking moments, sewn with delight,
Tickling my neck, oh what a sight!
It waves to my friends, a comical flare,
A vivid reminder of how much we care.

Sipping tea, it's a jester's parade,
Through potholes of life, it never did fade.
With puns and jest, it keeps me in stitches,
A leisurely ride on joy's fun glitches.

So gather 'round, let the laughter resound,
A fabric of friendship, in fun we're bound.
In grooves of nostalgia, our giggles entwined,
This woven delight is one of a kind!

An Embrace of Threads

Once it was new, bright colors ablaze,
Now a quirky relic with stories to praise.
Each frayed little corner has charmed its way,
Into the hearts that sport it each day.

With whispers of warmth on a chilly afternoon,
It dances and twirls, a fabric balloon.
Beware of the static, oh what a sight!
My hair like a porcupine, how funny, alright!

Stretched and pulled, it's a saucy tease,
Drawing all the eyes, like a comic breeze.
In the sun's embrace, it sparkles with cheer,
A playful companion, forever near.

So here's to our bond, lively and bright,
In laughter and colors, it's pure delight.
With each wrap, it promises giggles, sweet bread,
A joyous adventure in this tapestry thread!

Embraced in Fabric

A twist, a turn, a cozy hug,
Wrapped in warmth, like a snug bug.
It's slipped and slid into place,
Where's my phone? Oh, such a chase!

Poking out from every side,
A peekaboo game, it's hard to hide.
Does it match? Oh, what a joke,
Fashion faux pas, one big poke!

Colors clash, patterns collide,
Worn like armor, I won't subside.
It tickles me each time I move,
A bouncing ball, my fabric groove!

So here I stand, a sight to see,
Goofy looks, just let me be!
In every knot, a laugh set-free,
Fabric giggles, oh, just let me be!

Whispered Comfort

A gentle wrap, it hugs me tight,
Like a warm hug on a cold night.
It whispers secrets, soft and sweet,
Like a cheeky cat on my two feet!

It teases me with each small breeze,
Dancing round with foolish ease.
My snack tucked safe in its fold,
A grand reveal, I'm feeling bold!

Oh, how it flips and flops about,
Hiding crumbs, there's no doubt.
With a twirl and a joyful shout,
It's the best companion, let's go out!

Marvels made from threads and ties,
Fashion might bring tears to my eyes.
Yet, wrapped in this delightful mess,
I find true joy in my fabric dress!

Silken Encircling

Looped and tied in a playful fling,
A bright swirl, it makes me sing.
Like a merry-go-round for the silly,
I'm spinning round, oh so frilly!

It's a hug that likes to play peekaboo,
With every step, a giggle too.
I try to strut, it pulls me back,
A game of tag on a fabric track!

Colors bright, a rainbow's delight,
I'm a walking funhouse, what a sight!
Pulling me close, then letting me go,
A playful dance, just steal the show!

As I prance in my fabric swirl,
My mishaps cause a laugh-filled whirl.
Who knew that a wrap could be so fun?
In my own circus, I'm number one!

Shades of Serenity

A cloak of laughter wraps around,
In shades of silliness, I'm spellbound.
With every twirl, it takes a cue,
To waltz with me, a dance for two!

Each fold a giggle, every swirl a grin,
It's a joyful ride, let's begin!
It snores at night, tucked in my bed,
Pillow fights? Not on my head!

Colors clash in a vivid spree,
Unexpected matches as wild as can be.
This playful fabric, oh what a treat,
A whirlwind adventure — can't be beat!

So here I go, a lively show,
With whispers of fun and color glow.
In each embrace, laughter's balm,
My silly scarf, you hold me calm!

Binding Beyond Borders

A knot so tight, my neck does plead,
It's hugging me like I'm its steed.
Colors clash, a riotous sight,
Who knew warmth could start a fight?

Tangled tales, a twist or two,
It chased the cat, it danced with the dew.
An accessory with lofty dreams,
It's more than fabric, or so it seems!

Windy day, flair on parade,
Twirling around, my fashion charade.
Oh, how it flutters, all in jest,
This silly wrap, I must confess!

With whispers soft, it mocks my style,
Yet keeps me warm, oh what a trial!
A fashion faux pas, yet it stays,
In this snug hug, I'll find my ways.

Woven Whispers

Threads of laughter, stitched so bright,
It tickles my chin, what a delight!
A jester's garb, in rich array,
Swirling patterns, come what may!

Woven whispers, in the breeze,
It flirts and flutters with utmost ease.
Knotted loops that dance with glee,
"Who me? I'm fancy," says this spree!

A tug here, a twist there, oh no!
It just suggested a fashion show!
Beneath the sun, it takes its chance,
To show off its colors in a wild dance.

But when it's cold and I feel blue,
This playful wrap is my trusty crew.
In its embrace, oh what a fad,
A laugh, a smile—who could be sad?

Kisses of Cozy

A gentle nudge, a feathery kiss,
It wraps me up in snug bliss.
Cozy as a hug from a bear,
Yet sometimes it pulls my hair!

Rainy days, it's quite the charm,
It keeps the warmth and breaks the harm.
A sneeze or two, oh it must joke,
Causing fits of giggles and smoke!

Tangled with my favorite chair,
It brings a flair, a colorful scare.
What's this? A game in the wind?
My loyal splotch, my woven friend!

Though sometimes it trips, a graceful fall,
This cozy kiss, I can't recall.
With laughter bubbling, we'll face the cold,
In stitches and laughs, we'll be bold!

Harmonics of Heat

A symphony of warmth, I hear it hum,
With swirls and twirls, it's never glum.
A whimsical wrap, a playful tune,
It serenades me, morning to noon.

A funky dance in wardrobe's space,
It claims the spotlight, what a place!
Each note of fabric, a joyful ray,
While bugs join in, in their own way.

On chilly nights, by the fire's grace,
It wraps me tight, I've found my place.
Tickling my toes, a jolly kind,
Oh, the giggles that I can find!

Yet when I step out, it cannot tease,
An ochre edge swaying in the breeze.
With laughing hearts, we face the street,
In tunes of warmth, we can't be beat!

www.ingramcontent.com/pod-product-compliance
Lightning Source LLC
Chambersburg PA
CBHW070315120526
44590CB00017B/2688